Dr. John Polis

APOSTOLIC FUNCTIONS

Things Apostles Do

9 Apostolic Functions
Things Apostles Do
By John Polis

PAPERBACK ISBN: 978-1-7377236-7-7
Also available in HARDBACK and EBook editions

Prepared for Publication By

MAKING YOUR BOOK A REALITY

Cedar Point, NC | 843-929-8768 | info@BandBpublishingLLC.com

John Polis Ministries
600 The Drive
Fairmont, WV 26554
www.johnpolis.com

Printed in the United States of America.

CONTENTS

Chapter One

The Reality Of Apostles

"Therefore, holy brethren, partakers of the heavenly calling, consider the Apostle and High Priest of our confession, Christ Jesus, who was faithful to Him who appointed Him, as Moses also was faithful in all His house." Hebrews 3:1-2 NKJV

Here we find that Jesus is still operating in two official functions to His Body, Apostle and High Priest. As "Apostle," Jesus is still building His Church on planet earth. As "High Priest," He is representing us through His Precious Blood before the Throne of God. Apostles are builders of the Church (1 Corinthians 3:10) and are appointed such by God who has called and gifted them for the task.

In this passage we also see that Moses is compared to Christ Jesus as an "apostle" who was faithful to God as well in his assignment to "build the Church in the Wilderness"(Acts 7:38). Moses was the Old Testament "apostle" and Christ Jesus is the New Testament "Apostle" in this verse. An Old Testament passage that clearly illustrates the apostolic role of Moses is found in Exodus 39:42-43

> *"According to all that the Lord had commanded Moses, so the children of Israel did all the work. Then Moses looked over all the work, and indeed they had done it; as the Lord had commanded, just so they had done it. And Moses blessed them. Exodus 39:42-43 NKJV*

We see three apostolic functions laid out in this explanation of God's people at work to build the Tabernacle:

1. INSTRUCTION

"According to all that the Lord had commanded Moses." God gave Moses the instructions on how to build the Tabernacle, and Moses gave them to the people.

2. INSPECTION

"Then Moses looked over all the work." After the people had done the work as instructed, Moses inspected it to make sure it was as God had required.

2. IMPARTATION

"And Moses blessed them." The blessing of God was released upon the people as soon as Moses approved the work. This

is how God's order works in the building of His Church. The "blessing" imparted by God involved the manifestations of the Glory of God.

> *"...And he reared up the court round about the tabernacle and the altar, and set up the hanging of the court gate. So Moses finished the work. Then a cloud covered the tent of the congregation, and the glory of the Lord filled the tabernacle. And Moses was not able to enter into the tent of the congregation, because the cloud abode thereon, and the glory of the Lord filled the tabernacle. And when the cloud was taken up from over the tabernacle, the children of Israel went onward in all their journeys: But if the cloud were not taken up, then they journeyed not till the day that it was taken up. For the cloud of the Lord was upon the tabernacle by day, and fire was on it by night, in the sight of all the house of Israel, throughout all their journeys. Exodus 40:33-38 KJV*

God's intention for the Church today is to have the same supernatural manifestations of the glory of the Lord happening in our midst. There are five definite manifestations of the glory of God that we should expect today recorded in 1 Corinthians 10:1-4. Paul specifically states that these things were written for "our example" (verse 11).

> *"Moreover, brethren, I do not want you to be unaware that all our fathers were under the*

> *cloud, all passed through the sea, all were baptized into Moses in the cloud and in the sea, all ate the same spiritual food, and all drank the same spiritual drink. For they drank of that spiritual Rock that followed them, and that Rock was Christ." 1 Corinthians 10:1-4 NKJV*

The five supernatural manifestations include:

1. **Supernatural Deliverance** - “all passed through the sea”

2. **Supernatural Guidance** - “under the cloud”

3. **Supernatural Leadership** - ‘baptized into Moses”

4. **Supernatural Food** - “Manna”

5. **Supernatural Drink** - “living water from Christ.”

THE APOSTLES OF THE LAMB

> *“Now the names of the twelve apostles are these; The first, Simon, who is called Peter, and Andrew his brother; James the son of Zebedee, and John his brother; Philip, and Bartholomew; Thomas, and Matthew the publican; James the son of Alphaeus, and Lebbaeus, whose surname was Thaddaeus; Simon the Canaanite, and Judas Iscariot, who also betrayed him." Matthew 10:2-4 KJV*

> *"So Jesus said to them, "Assuredly I say to you, that in the regeneration, when the Son of Man sits on the throne of His glory, you who have followed Me will also sit on twelve thrones, judging the twelve tribes of Israel." Matthew 19:28 NKJV*

These twelve men were chosen by Jesus before His death and resurrection, in that sense they are unique apostles and cannot be duplicated for obvious reason. They will have this special place as Judges of Israel in the age to come according to Jesus because of their faithfulness to Him during His earthly ministry.

> *"But you are those who have continued with Me in My trials. And I bestow upon you a kingdom, just as My Father bestowed one upon Me, that you may eat and drink at My table in My kingdom, and sit on thrones judging the twelve tribes of Israel." Luke 22:28-30 NKJV*

The idea among some churches that "there are no apostles today" is the result of a dispensational teaching that relegates the supernatural aspects of Christianity to the "First Century Church" only. This erroneous teaching says that "apostles, signs, wonders and miracles" were only needed to "get the Church started" but are not needed today since the Church was began over 2000 years ago. We shall see that there are still apostles indeed in today's Church as well that are needed to continue "starting" the Church in the whole world and building it to maturity. The only difference between these "first" apostles is that they were chosen by Jesus before His death, but they have the same "gift of apostle" as the apostles chosen after His Resurrection.

THE ASCENSION APOSTLES

> *"But unto every one of us is given grace according to the measure of the gift of Christ. Wherefore he saith, When he ascended up on high, he led captivity captive, and gave gifts unto men..... And he gave some, apostles; and some, prophets; and some, evangelists; and some, pastors and teachers;" Ephesians 4:7, 8 & 11 KJV*

We see in these verses that Christ also gifted some as apostles after He ascended to the Father, These apostles have the same Holy Spirit enablement to do the work of apostles as the first twelve who were chosen by Christ before He left earth. Just like there is no difference in the prophets, teachers and evangelists that we read about in the Book of Acts with those in the church today, there is no difference in the "gift of apostle" either.

According to Apostle Paul, all five of these "ascension gifts" will be needed as long as the Church is on earth. Paul gives a "nine fold purpose" for these "fivefold gifts as follows:

- "for the equipping of the saints"
- "for the work of ministry"

- "for the edifying of the body of Christ"
- "till we all come to the unity of the faith"
- "and to the knowledge of the Son of God"
- "to a perfect man"
- "to the measure of the stature of the fullness of Christ;"

> *"that we should no longer be children...speaking the truth in love, may grow up in all things into Him who is the head—Christ" Ephesians 4:14-15 NKJV*

These fivefold gifts have been restored to the Church since the Protestant Reformation began in 1511 AD. In more recent years, since the late 1940's, the Church has begun to recognize and receive these gifts according to their actual function and name. The most recent of the gifts to be fully recognized were "prophet and apostle" (in that order). Previously, only the pastor, teacher and evangelist were understood clearly by the Church at large. The Bible teaches us that the "Hand of God" has five fingers which include the five gifts listed above.

> *"Humble yourselves therefore under the mighty hand of God, that he may exalt you in due time:" 1 Peter 5:6 KJV*

Peter is teaching the "younger men" in the Church at Rome not to be anxious about their callings, but to wait in submission to the Elders (1 Peter 5:1-5) until such time as they were fully qualified for leadership and subsequently appointment would come. The Eldership were fully functioning in the fivefold gifts, even Apostle Peter describes "himself" as an "elder" in these verses. In the Antioch Church, we see that the Eldership which presided over the appointment of Paul and Barnabas as "apostles" were "prophets and teachers."

> *"Now there were in the church that was at Antioch certain prophets and teachers; as Barnabas, and Simeon that was called Niger, and Lucius of Cyrene, and Manaen, which had been brought up with Herod the tetrarch, and Saul. As they ministered to the Lord, and fasted, the Holy Ghost said, Separate me Barnabas and Saul for the work whereunto I have called them. And when they had fasted and prayed, and laid their hands on them, they sent them away." Acts 13:1-3 KJV*

We know that the "arm of the Lord" must have a "hand" to release the power of the arm. If you have a great bicep in your arm with much strength, but have no hand on the arm, you have no way to use that power. God releases the power of His arm thru His Hand, which are the five ministry gifts of Ephesians 4:11. When we receive from these gifts, we receive the power of God into our lives, that is the reward God has for us.

> *"He that receiveth a prophet in the name of a prophet shall receive a prophet's reward..." Matthew 10:41a KJV*

By receiving the ministry gift as named, whether it is pastor, teacher, evangelist, prophet or apostle, we receive what God has given them for us, that is our reward. We will receive the revelation and anointing coming from each of these gifts and the nine fold purpose we mentioned earlier will happen in our lives. Our spiritual progress cannot be made apart from understanding and receiving these ministry gifts that Christ has sent to us to build the Church. Apostles and prophets are the foundation layers, the other gifts build upon the foundation that has been laid. (*For more detailed teaching on Ministry Gifts go to www.johnpolis.com*)

> *"And are built upon the foundation of the apostles and prophets, Jesus Christ himself being the chief corner stone; Ephesians 2:20 KJV*

Apostles and prophets work together to bring the "mystery of Christ" to the Church and reveal all the spiritual blessings (Ephesians 1:3) that we have inherited by being "in Christ." Pastors and teachers then take the revelation and break it down into "milk, meat and strong meat" to feed and grow the body of Christ. In this team model, apostles will deal more with establishing correct doctrine and character while prophets will deal more with recognizing spiritual gifts and callings. Although apostles and prophets can often times "switch roles," typically, apostles will deal more with the Word, while prophets will deal more with the Spirit. Usually, when the apostolic/prophetic team is operating, apostles will get "you to work for God" and prophets will "get God to work for you." When an apostolic/prophetic team is at work, you will go “deep in the Word” and “high in the Spirit.”

> *“Whereby, when ye read, ye may understand my knowledge in the mystery of Christ) Which in other ages was not made known unto the sons of men, as it is now revealed unto his holy apostles and prophets by the Spirit;" Ephesians 3:4-5 KJV*

This “mighty hand of God” has been illustrated in the following way for clarity,

- ***Apostles*** govern and are like the “thumb” which can work with all the other fingers.
- ***Prophets*** guide and are like the “pointing finger” of the hand.
- ***Evangelists*** gather and are like “the longest finger” for outreach.
- ***Pastors*** guard and are like the “wedding finger” that is preparing the bride for Christ.
- ***Teachers*** grow and are like the “littlest finger” because it is the only one that can open the ear.

MODERN DAY APOSTLES

There are many people recognized in today’s Church as “apostles” because of the fruit of ministry manifested in their lives. Some more recognized apostles would be Chuck Smith, Founder of Calvary Chapel; John Wimber, Founder of Vineyard Churches; C. Peter Wagner, Founder of The New Apostolic Reformation; John Kelly, Founder of International Coalition of Apostles, and Naomi Dowdy, Founder of Global Leadership Network.

Chapter Two

Function 1: Revelation

There are nine main characteristics of apostolic ministry that we will look at in some detail.

> *"And God has appointed these in the church: first apostles, second prophets, third teacherss..." 1 Corinthians 12:28 NKJV*

This verse shows a distinct order in God's unfolding strategy for His Church. The word "first" is the Greek word , "proton" and means "first in rank, order and importance." The Greek words for "second and third" are sequential and follow the apostle in rank, order and importance. When God is going to break a fresh revelation to the Church, He will begin with an apostle who usually will become a pioneer of that particular message to the body of Christ. The apostle will "*break the revelation*," the prophet will "*confirm the revelation*" and the teacher will "*explain the revelation*." The prophet is needed for confirmation by receiving the same revelation so that "by the mouth of two witnesses, every matter shall be established" (John 8:17; 2 Corinthians 13:1). We could use Martin Luther as an example of an apostle who was given a "fresh revelation" of "Justification by faith" (I say "fresh" because there are no "new" revelations apart from scripture), and became the leader of a movement that propagates his message to the world, the Lutheran Church. Church history records numerous others who rank among the apostles and have trumpeted a fresh word from God for the whole body of Christ to receive and grow thereby. These great apostolic leaders gave birth to our major Protestant denominations that all have a main truth that their particular movement espouses. If we take each of the truths revealed by these apostles that developed into the movements they led, and incorporate them into our lives, we will become the mature Church that Jesus is building. This truth is illustrated by the following verse from Psalms:

> *"There is a river, the streams whereof shall make glad the city of God, the holy place of the tabernacles of the most High. God is in the midst of her; she shall not be moved" Psalms 46:4-5 KJV*

This is prophetic of the Church out of which "flows the rivers of living water" (John 7:37-38). We see that there are "streams" that "flow together" to make the "river." These streams are the "revelations" received by the apostles for the Church, each one "building upon another" (Isaiah 28:10) until the Church reaches "full stature" in Christ. God never intended the truth to divide the Church into all of the different groups we see today, even though God uses these organizations for His purpose. God intends that "*he that has an ear to hear, will hear what the Spirit is saying to the Church,*" and will not be hindered by any denominational name tags from receiving the truth into our lives. We are told that we can,

> *"Let the word of Christ dwell in you richly in all wisdom; teaching and admonishing one another..." Colossians 3:16 KJV*

An illustration that shows how the apostle first receives a fresh truth for the Church and then it is taken by the other ministry gifts to explain and expound upon, is found in John's Gospel with the story of the Feeding of the Five Thousand.

> *"When Jesus then lifted up his eyes, and saw a great company come unto him, he saith unto Philip, Whence shall we buy bread, that these may eat? And this he said to prove him: for he himself knew what he would do. Philip answered him, Two hundred pennyworth of bread is not sufficient for them, that every one of them may take a little. One of his disciples, Andrew, Simon Peter's brother, saith unto him, There is a lad here, which hath five barley loaves, and two small fishes: but what are they among so*

> *many? And Jesus said, Make the men sit down. Now there was much grass in the place. So the men sat down, in number about five thousand. And Jesus took the loaves; and when he had given thanks, he distributed to the disciples, and the disciples to them that were set down; and likewise of the fishes as much as they would."*
> *John 6:5-11 KJV*

Jesus, as the "apostle" in His earthly ministry, blessed the food and gave it to His disciples to distribute to the crowd. Is this not a clear illustration of how the fivefold ministry gifts work in the Church today? As the apostles receive the fresh manna, and the prophet confirms it, the other gifts then receive it for mass distribution to the whole body of Christ. This also shows the importance of recognizing and receiving from apostles today, or we could find ourselves becoming an "old wineskin" just living from yesterday's revelation.

Chapter Three

Function 2: Ordination

> *"And when they had ordained them elders in every church, and had prayed with fasting, they commended them to the Lord, on whom they believed." Acts 14:23 KJV*

As Paul and Barnabas traveled together to strengthen the churches, they trained and ordained leaders for each congregation they either started or found already in existence. The leaders were called "elders" (presbuteros meaning "not a novice") because they represented what a "mature believer" in Christ should exemplify to other Christians. Becoming an elder in a local church is not a matter of having a "gift" or "anointing" only, but of having the Christ-like character that will inspire other believers to grow accordingly. What really qualifies one for ministry is not just being "gifted," but being an "*example to the flock of God*" (1 Peter 5:1-4). When one who is in leadership at this level fails to "role model" the qualities listed as requirements for eldership in 1 Timothy 3:1-8 and Titus 1:5-8, they should be relieved of their leadership responsibilities until such time as they make the necessary changes to re-qualify as an elder again. One grave mistake made by today's church that was not permitted in the early church, is that of leaving a "disqualified leader" in authority simply because they still manifest the "anointing." We must remember that the "gifts and callings of God are irrevocable" (Romans 11:29) but "ordination" is not irrevocable. When God gives someone a gift, He doesn't ever take it back, but He may limit the use of that gift due to failure to manifest the necessary character to coincide with the gift and call.

When one manifests the "anointing," attention will be drawn to that person because the anointing attracts. People are often taken by the gifts and personality of an individual before they have found out exactly what kind of life the person is living. I tell future leaders that "*when you are publicly set forth for ministry, it will be because the people drawn to your gift will not be disappointed by a lack of character when they get close enough to examine your life.*" This is why the New Testament teaches a message of discipleship, the "*apostles*" were first "*disciples*" of Jesus where they learned not just how he "ministered" but how he "lived." When Jesus was assured that His followers fully understood how He expected them to live, and to minister, He was released to go to the Cross.

> *"A disciple is not above his teacher, but everyone who is perfectly trained will be like his teacher."*
> *Luke 6:40 NKJV*

Any believer can exercise his gifts in daily life as they go about, and may manifest a strong anointing in leading others to Christ, praying for the sick or prophesying. However, to exercise one's gifts publicly as an "official" in the church, where others begin to look to a person for "leadership," can only be done when one has met the qualifications outlined in Scripture for such functions, and having been properly recognized by those in spiritual authority.

There are warnings regarding placing people into leadership roles based upon gift and calling alone, and not spiritual maturity.

"*Do not lay hands on anyone hastily*" meaning "prematurely" or before someone is mature enough to lead by example. (1 Timothy 5:22a NKJV) This passage is referring to "ordaining" a person into a leadership role in the church.

The disciples were taken through rigorous training by the Lord Jesus for over three years where they were with him nearly day and night. They experienced all that He was going thru, saw Him in all aspects of ministry, and learned the "heart of the Father" from Him. When it would be "their turn" at ministry, they would be doing it for the right reasons and with the Father's heart for the people. They would be following the Holy Spirit as Jesus did in His earthly ministry of power, and continuing in "*all that Jesus began both to do and teach.*" *Acts 1:1-2 NKJV*

Ordination was the last step in a process that we see outlined so clearly in Matthew's Gospel. There are six steps that Jesus walked his "students of ministry" through that we must all follow before being "released" into a leadership role in God's Church. These are the same steps all disciples must follow in order to fulfill any God given destiny and purpose, in or outside of the Church.

1. SELECTION

Matthew 4:19, Jesus called certain individuals to come into a training relationship with Himself. He will call every "believer" to become His "disciple."

2. INSTRUCTION

Matthew 5-7, Jesus took them up on the mountain and taught them the Word of God. The "Beatitudes" were the character qualities of Christ.

3. OBSERVATION

Matthew 8-9, Jesus took them into the place of ministry with Him where they saw Him at work. "He turned to His disciples who were with Him." Matthew 8:10

4. DELEGATION

Matthew 10, Jesus called the disciples together and gave them power and authority for a special assignment for which He held them accountable. Mark 6:30

5. CORRECTION

Matthew 17, Jesus corrected them when they could not do what He had told them to do because of "unbelief."

6. ORDINATION

Matthew 28, After His resurrection, Jesus gave them authority and commissioned (ordained) them to carry on in His place. They now were publicly recognized as the leaders of the New Testament Church.

Ordination or "appointment" to ministry should be done by recognized spiritual authority, such as the Apostles were in the New Testament. In the Kingdom of God, all authority is delegated from a higher authority with Jesus Christ as the Head (or highest in authority). We are speaking here mainly of ordination to "official functions" within the local church as Deacons and Elders or Bishops. Even if someone is beginning a ministry outside the local church, such as in the Marketplace where an "ordination" is not necessary, they should still have been through a period of discipleship with mature leadership so that they may manifest the wisdom and character of Christ to the world.

> *"And whatsoever ye do in word or deed, do all in the name of the Lord Jesus, giving thanks to God and the Father by him" Colossians 3:17 KJV*

Apostles are responsible in today's church, as in the early church to make sure that the highest standards of leadership are maintained, and that only those who meet the qualifications for public ministry are permitted to enter the holy office. Apostles themselves are to be the supreme example of the highest standards for others to follow, as Paul reminded the believers of Thessalonica.

> *(verse 10)"You are witnesses, and God also, how devoutly and justly and blamelessly we behaved ourselves among you who believe; (verse 11) as you know how we exhorted, and comforted, and charged every one of you, as a father does his own children (verse 12) that you would walk worthy of God who calls you into His own kingdom and glory." 1 Thessalonians 2:10-12 NKJV*

The following verses outline the apostolic strategy of Paul for raising up strong Christians.

- The EXAMPLE of APOSTOLIC MINISTRY - verse 10 devoutly | justly | blamelessly
- The FUNCTION of APOSTOLIC MINISTRY - verse 11 exhorted | comforted | charged
- The RESULT of APOSTOLIC MINISTRY - verse 12 Walking Worthy of God in Kingdom glory

The purpose of "ordination" is to insure that the proper examples of leadership in Christian ministry are maintained. Those who qualify for ordination should realize that the standards they were required to show forth to receive ordination, are the same standards that must be maintained in order to retain their ordination. Therefore, it is necessary that everyone remain in the spiritual relationships that God has established for them so that accountability can be maintained. This is how authority is maintained in ministry. Authority, responsibility and accountability cannot be separated. Authority in ministry doesn't come from the "anointing," which is the "ability" to minister. Authority comes from "appointment" or "ordination" which should guarantee that the gifted person is also a mature and exemplary person. A misunderstanding of this truth is the reason for chaos in ministry, church splits and disillusionment among Christians. Lawlessness, or "becoming a law unto ourselves" with no accountability "except to the Lord," was not permitted in the New Testament Church. *Everyone* was accountable to *someone* as we read scripture, those who refused to align properly with God ordained authority were marked as rebellious and troublemakers, regardless of how "gifted" they were. The Word of God teaches,

> *"Let all things be done decently and in order." 1 Corinthians 14:40 KJV*

Many times when people insist on "ministering" without being related to spiritual authority, it is due to ignorance of Biblical principle. These sincere people can be corrected with teaching. Then there are those who are immature and adolescent in thinking who want to "try their wings" without anyone "controlling" them. These people just need a little time to grow up into a more mature understanding of how God's order for ministry works. But, those who claim to be mature, and have sat under correct teaching on these matters, but still refuse to submit themselves to godly authority, are to be avoided as "maverick sheep" who will lead others into a rebellious lifestyle of division in the church.

> *"Obey those who rule (lead) over you, and be submissive, for they watch out for your souls, as those who must give account. Let them do so with joy and not with grief, for that would be unprofitable for you." Hebrews 13:17 NKJV*

Chapter Four

Function 3: Foundation

> *"According to the grace of God which was given to me, as a wise master builder I have laid the foundation, and another builds on it. But let each one take heed how he builds on it." 1 Corinthians 3:10 NKJV*

Paul describes an aspect of his apostolic ministry as "laying foundation" for others to build upon. Principles that apply to building the Church "universal," also apply to building the Church "local," and to the individual Christian who is also the "temple of the Holy Spirit." 1 Corinthians 6:19-20 Paul refers to himself as a "wise master builder," a phrase which has important implications. Those without apostolic gifting may not see the importance of certain foundational principles when they set out to build the church, especially the local church. Often times the emphasis is on "church growth" and how to survive in the "church market" with the consumer mentality prevailing in the minds of many Christians who are looking for the church offering the best "return on the dollar," and the most exciting programs. Pastors may be pressured to build for "success," rather than a New Testament model of a believer in Christ. Being in a hurry for growth can lead to overlooking the principles that will insure the local church will be around for the "long haul," still converting and discipling people for more than one generation. That is why Paul emphasizes building "wisely." The foundation of a fruitful church or Christian will have the following principles established within.

1. DOCTRINAL FOUNDATION

"Therefore leaving the principles of the doctrine of Christ, let us go on unto perfection; not laying again the foundation of repentance from dead works, and of faith toward God, Of the doctrine of baptisms, and of laying on of hands, and of resurrection of the dead, and of eternal judgment." Hebrews 6:1-2 KJV

Paul emphasized the "first principles" of Christ, or the things Christians should be learning first after conversion to the faith. It is not wise building to jump into the "deep things of God" without the proper understanding of the basics, or milk of the Word (1 Peter 2:1-2). Every church should have a regular class for new believers that cover these essentials of the Christian faith, before moving on to the more mature messages.

Every believer should have a comprehensive "Christology," whereby they can explain the Person and Work of Jesus Christ including his Pre-existence; Incarnation, Substitutionary Work; Resurrection and Literal Bodily Return. Paul warned the believers about those preaching "another Jesus whom we have not preached" (2 Corinthians 11:4). Every believer must be able to help people "meet the Biblical Jesus" and refute the false teachings that are seducing many and blinding their minds to the Truth.

Understanding what I call "Big Bible Words" is essential for all believers to learn in the first year or two of their new life in Christ. A "Big Bible Word" is a word often used in scripture like Faith, Grace, Righteousness, Love, Prayer, Holy, Wisdom, or Peace. When God talks a lot about a subject, we should also.

Believers should also understand key "theological terms" such as Justification, Regeneration, Sanctification, Glorification, Revelation and Retribution. Paul warns of the necessity of establishing believers in "sound doctrine" that will enable them to remain steadfast in the faith when the time comes that "sound doctrine" will be assailed.

> *"For the time will come when they will not endure sound doctrine, but according to their own desires, because they have itching ears, they will heap up for themselves teachers; and*

they will turn their ears away from the truth, and be turned aside to fables. 2 Timothy 4:3-4 NKJV

2. PRAYER FOUNDATION

Apostles are people of prayer above all things, they are mighty intercessors that stand in the gap for the people of God at all times, as we gather from Paul's writings.

> *"For this cause we also, since the day we heard it, do not cease to pray for you" Colossians 1:9 KJV*

> *"Night and day praying exceedingly that we might see your face, and might perfect that which is lacking in your faith?" 1 Thessalonians 3:10 KJV*

> *"And they continued stedfastly in the apostles' doctrine and fellowship, and in breaking of bread, and in prayers." Acts 2:42 KJV*

The apostles didn't just teach prayer to the saints, they modeled prayer to them. Just like Jesus did with the twelve disciples, the early apostles not only started all the prayer meetings, but they continued to attend and lead in prayer so that the saints could hear the heart of someone praying who understands the will and purpose of God. When the disciples prayed with Jesus, they heard him praying what was in the heart of the Father. Praying with apostles is a life changing experience for believers and they should seek for every opportunity to be in the atmosphere that is pregnant with apostolic anointing.

A prayer foundation includes an understanding of all different kinds of prayer so that the church is skilled in the art of prayer.

> *"praying always with all prayer and supplication in the Spirit, being watchful to this end with all perseverance and supplication for all the saints" Ephesians 6:18 NKJV*

- **Intercessory prayer** - this includes praying the purposes of God for individuals, organizations, cities, states and nations, and may be done in a known language or in other tongues. 1 Corinthians 14:14-15

- **Petition prayer** - this includes making a request known to God based upon the revealed will of God in scripture or from the Holy Spirit to an individual. 1 John 5:14-15

- **Prayer of committal** - this involves committing something or someone to God for the working out of His Divine plan. Proverbs 3:5-6

- **Prayer in the spirit** - this is praying in tongues to build up your inner man and become more sensitive to Holy Spirit within. This is a powerful tool for obtaining guidance from the Lord, and revelation of the Word.

- **Prayer of Faith** - this is the prayer to be used in praying for the sick, and for any personal desire. (James 5:14-16; Mark 11:24)

3. FINANCIAL FOUNDATION

The apostles taught the importance of giving and receiving in the area of finances.

> *"Now you Philippians know also that in the beginning of the gospel, when I departed from Macedonia, no church shared with me concerning giving and receiving but you only. Philippians 4:15 NKJV*

Teaching proper financial stewardship is the basis for all Divine supply in a ministry or the life of a believer. All should understand the difference between, First fruits, Tithes, Offerings and Alms. Also, the importance of financing ministry apart from contributions is part of the apostolic message. Apostles operate with a "kingly" anointing and are often successful business men as well as ministry leaders. Paul's example of "tent making" to provide for his own needs gave him the freedom to minister anywhere at any time without dependence on the church's giving.

First fruits

> *"The firstfruits of your grain and your new wine and your oil, and the first of the fleece of your sheep, you shall give him." Deuteronomy 18:4 NKJV*

> *"Honor the Lord with your wealth, with the first fruits of all your crops; then your barns will be filled to overflowing, and your vats will brim with new wine." Proverbs 3:9-10 NIV*

Any time you receive increase in your life, the first "taste" belongs to God. For example, if you received a raise on your job resulting in $50 additional per week, and you were paid twice monthly, your first check would have $100 increase in it. This $100 is the "first fruits" and belongs to God.

Tithe

> *"And all the tithe of the land, whether of the seed of the land, or of the fruit of the tree, is the Lord's: it is holy unto the Lord." Leviticus 27:30 KJV*

The "tithe" means "one tenth." Tithing is much more than just an "amount," it involves a "place" and a "purpose" that is designated by God just like the amount is designated by God and cannot be "negotiated" by circumstances, it "*belongs to the Lord.*"

> *""Will a man rob God? Yet you have robbed Me! But you say, 'In what way have we robbed You?' In tithes and offerings. You are cursed with a curse, For you have robbed Me, Even this whole nation. Bring all the tithes into the storehouse, That there may be food in My house, And try Me now in this," Says the Lord of hosts, "If I will not*

open for you the windows of heaven And pour out for you such blessing That there will not be room enough to receive it. "And I will rebuke the devourer for your sakes, So that he will not destroy the fruit of your ground, Nor shall the vine fail to bear fruit for you in the field," Says the Lord of hosts; "And all nations will call you blessed, For you will be a delightful land," Says the Lord of hosts." Malachi 3:8-12 NKJV

- ***Amount of the tithe - one tenth.*** Should we pay God before we pay Caesar? Tithing from the "gross income" means the "gross is blessed."

- ***Place of the tithe - the storehouse.*** Represents the place food was stored for the priests. We are the holy priesthood of the Lord now as born again people, our food is stored in the local church were the ministry gifts are anointed to "feed the flock."

- ***Purpose of the tithe - "that there may be food in my house."*** The ministry of the Word of God is provided for thru the tithe.

Blessing of the tithe - is threefold.

1. ***Precipitation*** - the windows of heaven open and rain falls on your life. Nothing grows without water.

2. ***Protection*** - the devourer is rebuked.

3. ***Productivity*** - you shall be a delightsome land.

Who would not want these blessings from the Lord?

Alms - "generosity towards the poor motivated by compassion."

> *"He that hath pity upon the poor lendeth unto the Lord; and that which he hath given will he pay him again." Proverbs 19:17 KJV*

The Lord promises to reimburse you for the alms you have given to the poor.

Offering - "seed sowing" because the offering is returned in multiplied amount.

> *"Give, and it shall be given unto you; good measure, pressed down, and shaken together, and running over, shall men give into your bosom. For with the same measure that ye mete withal it shall be measured to you again. Luke 6:38 KJV*

> *"Moreover it is required in stewards, that a man be found faithful." 1 Corinthians 4:2 KJV*

Ministry leaders should seek to have a "financial council" and not just be the "final word" on the finances of the ministry. Those handling the ministry income should be trained in bookkeeping and Non Profit Tax Laws. Whcn thc ministry is small and getting started, it may be necessary to seek help from larger ministries whom they are in relationship with for coaching people who work in the financial department. A budget should be implemented immediately to insure that finances flow into the vision of the ministry with percentages based upon the priority of each item in the budget. Eventually, when the ministry begins to grow and resources increase, regular audits should be professionally completed yearly. Following these basic protocols for finances will insure that integrity is maintained and that no one is "going to jail."

4. LEADERSHIP FOUNDATION

A ministry that is built wisely upon apostolic foundations will have a training program for future leaders. Wisdom dictates that "quality demands qualifications," that is why the New Testament gives qualifications for leadership in the local church including Deacon, Elders and Bishops. Every ministry should include what is called a "ladder of leadership" so that those who have the "desire to aspire" can climb higher in responsibility and influence within the ministry they serve. Leadership guru, John Maxwell states that *"the measure of a church is not the number of followers it produces, but the number of leaders." Titus 1:5-8; 1 Timothy 3:1-10*

The senior leader of a local church should be trained in a threefold job description that includes:

- **FEEDING THE FLOCK** - making sure that the proper spiritual diet is met and that a preaching calendar is planned for the church based upon the perceived needs of people, doctrinal teaching and discipleship.

- **MANAGING THE FLOCK** - making use of the human resources that God has provided by placing people in positions based upon their gifts, passion and personality.

- **LEADING THE FLOCK** - having a clear vision from God, purpose and mission statement. Leadership is the ability to cast vision and incorporate people into the vision. A successful leader must be able to change as changes in culture occur around us, not changing the "content" of the message but the methods of communicating it.

5. WORSHIP FOUNDATION

The Presence of God can be accessed by the believer individually or by the church corporately thru Thanksgiving, Praise and Worship. Foundational to a thriving spiritual life and culture is learning to cultivate an atmosphere that welcomes the manifest Presence of God.

> *"Make a joyful noise unto the Lord, all the earth: make a loud noise, and rejoice, and sing praise. Sing unto the Lord with the harp; with the harp, and the voice of a psalm. With trumpets and sound of cornet make a joyful noise before the Lord, the King." Psalm 98:4-6 KJV*

Regardless of the gifts and talents of people involved in the worship ministry, the most important thing is not the "preparation of the music," but the "preparation of the worshipper." Those involved in leading others into God's

Presence must have first cultivated their own “secret place” where they encounter God intimately in private worship. Then when they appear before the people to lead them in worship, they will lead by example as they enter the “glory” they are accustomed to experiencing. The worship ministry can become too “theatrical” empty of God’s glory unless those involved on the stage are “true worshippers” themselves.

These five areas are vital in laying a wise foundation in our lives and ministries.

Chapter Five

Function 4: Inspection

"For though I be absent in the flesh, yet am I with you in the spirit, joying and beholding your order, and the stedfastness of your faith in Christ." Colossians 2:5 KJV

As the founder of this church, Paul performed regular inspections of their spiritual life and the flow of ministry among them. Apostles are "inspectors" of the church as we see in this verse, looking for the signs of life and fruitfulness. The Greek word translated "bishop" has this meaning, "to inspect, to superintend," the apostles functioned as "overseers" of the churches and trained others to do this work as well. Paul gives instructions to the elders at Ephesus to "oversee the flock of God."

> *"Take heed therefore unto yourselves, and to all the flock, over the which the Holy Ghost hath made you overseers, to feed the church of God, which he hath purchased with his own blood."*
> *Acts 20:28 KJV*

Apostles that have founded churches have the responsibility to provide oversight to the congregations as their "spiritual fathers" and are referred to as "vertical apostles" because they are "over them in the Lord." The following scriptures give a picture of Paul's paternal care of the Corinthians.

> *"I write not these things to shame you, but as my beloved sons I warn you. For though ye have ten thousand instructers in Christ, yet have ye not many fathers: for in Christ Jesus I have begotten you through the gospel. Wherefore I beseech you, be ye followers of me. For this cause have I sent unto you Timotheus, who is my beloved son, and faithful in the Lord, who shall bring you into remembrance of my ways which be in Christ, as I teach every where in every church."*
> *1 Corinthians 4:14-17 KJV*

Apostles may give oversight upon request to a ministry they have not personally founded, not as an "overseer" to them, but more of a consulting figure. These types of apostolic relationships may be referred to as "horizontal apostles" who serve in an "apostolic helps" to churches and ministries, but are not looked upon as the "father" of the ministry. A more modern term is "coaching" or "mentoring."

We see an example of our Chief Apostle, the Lord Jesus Christ, as he performs an "apostolic inspection" on the Seven Churches of Asia found in Revelation 3-4. Here the Lord, corrects, affirms, reproves and instructs all seven churches as needed. Apostolic inspection will often include one or all of these aspects. As noted in Colossians 2:5, the overseeing apostle does not need to be present "in flesh" in order to know what the condition of the flock is, but may know it by revelation of the Spirit since the church or ministry is within the sphere of responsibility of that apostle. In the following verses, Paul shows the limits of his authority and claims that the Corinthians are indeed part of his "apostolic sphere." Paul would be looking for the things mentioned above under "Foundation" when he inspected the churches under his care.

> *"For we are not overextending ourselves (as though our authority did not extend to you), for it was to you that we came with the gospel of Christ; not boasting of things beyond measure, that is, in other men's labors, but having hope, that as your faith is increased, we shall be greatly enlarged by you in our sphere, to preach the gospel in the regions beyond you, and not to boast in another man's sphere of accomplishment." 2 Corinthians 10:14-16 NKJV*

Allowing for godly and seasoned leadership to inspect our lives and ministries is the characteristic of a "sincere heart" before the Lord. Godly and seasoned leaders will have the best interest of the people and churches they are serving as they seek to point out both the strengths and weaknesses that need to be addressed. Paul said to the Corinthians, and to all of us,

> *"Let all things be done unto edifying." 1 Corinthians 14:26b KJV*

Jesus not only performed apostolic inspections on churches as noted above, but on individuals as well. In the story of the Rich Young Ruler, Jesus reveals to this young man the "one thing" that is keeping him from obtaining his desire.

> *"And when he was gone forth into the way, there came one running, and kneeled to him, and asked him, Good Master, what shall I do that I may inherit eternal life? And Jesus said unto him, Why callest thou me good? there is none good but one, that is, God. Thou knowest the commandments, Do not commit adultery, Do not kill, Do not steal, Do not bear false witness, Defraud not, Honour thy father and mother. And he answered and said unto him, Master, all these have I observed from my youth. Then Jesus beholding him loved him, and said unto him, One thing thou lackest: go thy way, sell whatsoever thou hast, and give to the poor, and thou shalt have treasure in heaven: and come, take up the cross, and follow me." Mark 10:17-21 KJV*

This passage reveals the heart of the Master as He seeks to guide this individual to "breakthrough" in his life. Those seasoned apostolic leaders will follow the example and spirit of Jesus as they seek to serve God's redeemed people. Notice the progression of spirit led ministry thru Jesus to this potential disciple.

"*Then Jesus, LOOKING at him...*" (verse 21a) We inspect by "looking" at something. As Jesus looked at him with an anointed gaze, the Spirit of God showed him by revelation what the "one thing" lacking was. Jesus saw into this man's heart.

."*...LOVED him,*" (verse 21a) When Jesus saw the issue that needed addressed, His heart was touched with love for the young man, is this not the real motive of all ministry. But Jesus didn't stop there with Looking at and Loving the man, because real love will always do what is best for the other person.

."*.and SAID to him..*"(verse 21a) Jesus LAID IT OUT for him in plain terms exactly what his problem was, and how he could solve it. This is the best illustration of apostolic inspection of an individual I have ever seen. Seasoned apostles "see with revelation," "are motivated by love," and "give the person what they need most."

Chapter Six

Function 5: Expansion

> *"But ye shall receive power, after that the Holy Ghost is come upon you: and ye shall be witnesses unto me both in Jerusalem, and in all Judaea, and in Samaria, and unto the uttermost part of the earth." Acts 1:8 KJV*

A great man of God once said, "*The light that shines the farthest, shines the brightest at home.*" Jesus said, "Jerusalem first," this would be the site of the Holy Spirit explosion that would shake the world to the core. But it didn't stop there, it spread like a concentric circle in ever widening circumference to take in the whole known world.

> *"These that have turned the world upside down are come hither also;" Acts 17:6b KJV*

Apostles are gifted to see very far off, they are visionaries who can imagine the whole world under the influence of the Kingdom of God, and they labor to that end. An apostolic leader will never be content to "maintain a good ministry" and "just keep the doors open," but will always be looking for ways and means to reach the unreached and tell the untold. Apostles are "adventurers" of the Spirit, risk takers and pioneers. Apostles have a "gift of faith" for expansion of the Kingdom of God that will rattle the minds of people listening to the plans, and the cost of those plans that they will most likely have to share in providing as God leads them. When others get content to "rest on our laurels" and get comfortable with our achievements, the apostle is there to expand our horizon and show us another battle to be fought and mountain to be taken for God's glory.

As an Apostle Himself, Jesus left us with the vision of world expansion and the instructions on how to accomplish the goal.

THE GREAT COMMISSION

"And He said to them, "Go into all the world and preach the gospel to every creature. He who believes and is baptized will be saved; but he who does not believe will be condemned. And these signs will follow those who believe: In My name they will cast out demons; they will speak with new tongues; they will take up serpents; and if they drink anything deadly, it will by no means hurt them; they will lay hands on the sick, and they will recover." Mark 16:15-18 NKJV

> *"And Jesus came and spake unto them, saying, All power is given unto me in heaven and in earth. Go ye therefore, and teach all nations, baptizing them in the name of the Father, and of the Son, and of the Holy Ghost: Teaching them to observe all things whatsoever I have commanded you: and, lo, I am with you always, even unto the end of the world. Amen. Matthew 28:18-20 KJV*

The apostolic strategy is clear, "*preach and teach the Word of God with supernatural manifestations of the Spirit accompanying.*" This was the purpose of "the Holy Spirit coming upon you," to empower the church to complete the assignment by preaching, teaching, healing and delivering people worldwide. The distinction in the two aspects of the Great Commission is that "preaching is announcing the facts of the gospel" and "teaching is explaining the facts of the gospel." Paul followed this strategy closely in his apostolic ministry of expansion as recorded in the following verse.

> *"Whom we preach, warning every man, and teaching every man in all wisdom; that we may present every man perfect in Christ Jesus: Whereunto I also labour, striving according to his working, which worketh in me mightily." Colossians 1:28-29 KJV*

When apostles are in leadership of the Church, the Church will have the right vision, and understand their purpose in the world. God is restoring the apostolic gift to the Church in this generation so that the greatest harvest among the nations is yet before us. The Kingdom of God comes to maturity on earth in three stages according to the teaching of Jesus in Mark 4:26-28, "first the blade, then the corn, then the full corn in the ear." In terms of the progress of the Church toward maturity, we could say "the Evangelical Movement has a vision to save sinners from hell to heaven," "the Charismatic Movement has a vision to live the abundant life on earth," but the "Apostolic Movement has a vision to transform the world." Expansion is the message of the apostle.

Chapter Seven

Function 6: Correction

Dealing with difficult people and situations is something every apostle is equipped to do, even though it may never become a function that one is fully comfortable performing. The Epistles give us several types of difficult people and scenarios that needed addressed with apostolic wisdom. Not the least of which was the case of "incest" found among the Corinthian believers.

> *"For I indeed, as absent in body but present in spirit, have already judged (as though I were present) him who has so done this deed. In the name of our Lord Jesus Christ, when you are gathered together, along with my spirit, with the power of our Lord Jesus Christ, deliver such*

> *a one to Satan for the destruction of the flesh, that his spirit may be saved in the day of the Lord Jesus." 1 Corinthians 5:3-5 NJKV*

What stands out most about this immoral situation is the length of time it was known about, but not dealt with by the eldership present. Corinth was at this time having a great move of the Spirit as we read in Chapters 12-14, but was apparently not paying attention to the ungodly lifestyles of many of the "saints." It is interesting that there were "prophets and teachers" present in the church locally who were conducting the meetings where the Gifts of the Spirit flowed freely (1 Corinthians 1:7) and miracles were a common happening. This neglect of the moral condition existing in the church could be due to the focus of the leading ministry gifts. Prophets are more given to the "manifestations of the Spirit" and are often involved in "recognizing and activating gifts and callings" in the believer. Teachers are focused on "getting people into the Word" and explaining the scriptures to everyone. While we are getting people deeper in the Word and higher in the Spirit, we can sometimes overlook the need for character development in the believers as well. In an exciting atmosphere like they were having in Corinth, it could be easy to allow certain behavior to exist and allow people to remain in a carnal state regarding spiritual growth.

> *"And I, brethren, could not speak unto you as unto spiritual, but as unto carnal, even as unto babes in Christ. I have fed you with milk, and not with meat: for hitherto ye were not able to*

> *bear it, neither yet now are ye able. For ye are yet carnal: for whereas there is among you envying, and strife, and divisions, are ye not carnal, and walk as men?" 1 Corinthians 3:1-3 KJV*

This is similar to the problems existing in the church following the Charismatic Renewal where much emphasis was put on the move of the Spirit and teaching of the Word with little regard to the lifestyle of the believers. The church remained carnal for many years while enjoying the move of God, until the apostolic anointing began to be released and more teaching on the character of the believer began to be emphasized again. Paul often spoke of his character before his gifts.

> *"Paul, a servant of God, and an apostle of Jesus Christ," Titus 1:1 KJV*

Apostles will not neglect to confront issues that have potential to destroy the individual and the church corporately. It is for this reason that they are often the target of accusations as Jesus was for "exposing the sins of the religious leaders" in his day. Most people would prefer the prophet to activate their gifts, or the teacher to explain mysteries, rather than an apostle to correct ungodly beliefs and behaviors. But we must have all the gifts impacting us if we are to "*Grow up in all aspects into Him who is the Head, even Christ." Ephesians 4:15 NKJV*

Some of the difficult people we find mentioned in the New

Testament that we are given instruction on dealing with are listed below:

- **Evil men and seducers** - *2 Thessalonians 3:1-2 "He requested prayer for deliverance from these men."*
- **Unthankful** - *Luke 6:35 "Be kind to the unthankful."*
- **Divisive** - *Romans 16:17 "Avoid and mark them."*
- **Offensive** - *Matthew 18:15 "Confront them."*
- **Unruly** - *1 Thessalonians 5:14 "Warn them."*
- **Disobedient** - *1 Peter 3:1 "Show them."*
- **Opposers of themselves** - *2 Timothy 2:24-26 "Instruct them."*
- **Homosexuals** - *Romans 1:29-32 "Knowing the judgment of God."*

Apostles have the grace to confront whatever is not in keeping with the truth of the Word of God. Paul even confronted his fellow apostle, Peter, for compromising the Word (Galatians 2:11-16) of Grace when he withdrew from fellowship from the Gentile converts for fear of the Jews who had come from James to see what was happening under Peter's ministry. There is a great need today for confrontation of false teaching and unbiblical standards among leaders, which is the responsibility of apostles. The Jerusalem Council of the early church was comprised of "*apostles and elders*" (Acts 15:6) who were to settle disputes and maintain the standard of faith "*once delivered to the saints*" (Jude 3). Making things "correct" is the job of all leadership gifts, but primarily of apostles. I am not talking about being a "god player" in the lives of others, but to "*continue all that Jesus began both to do and teach.*" Acts 1:1-2 NKJV

Confronting problems and problem people is often avoided as people seek to "keep everyone happy" so that no one leaves the church and takes their money with them. Also, many sincere leaders have been so wounded by the "backlash" from people full of "malice and wickedness" (1 Corinthians 5:8), that they have chosen to avoid making a scenario that could result in more emotional pain and trauma in their own lives. However, to allow the spread of evil in our midst will ultimately result in greater loss and problems. Paul told Timothy to prepare for times of stress in ministry and develop the endurance necessary to walk in the apostolic calling. Paul uses three strong words to prepare his "son" Timothy for dealing with the challenges an apostle must face.

> *"Preach the word; be instant in season, out of season; reprove, rebuke, exhort with all long suffering and doctrine." 2 Timothy 4:2 KJV*

> *"But watch thou in all things, endure afflictions, do the work of an evangelist, make full proof of thy ministry." 2 Timothy 4:5 KJV*

- "***reprove***" - meaning to "convict, convince, tell a fault." (call it what it is, sin is sin).

- "***rebuke***" - meaning to censure or admonish; by implication, forbid.

- "***exhort***" - to call near, to invite.

This is a very interesting sequence that could sound like this, "*Tell a fault, forbid it, and invite people to draw near to God.*" If we are not careful, we tell people to "draw near to God" without telling them that they must avoid certain behavior as part of coming close to Him. Another apostle said it similarly.

> *"Draw near to God and He will draw near to you. Cleanse your hands, you sinners; and purify your hearts, you double-minded." James 4:8 NKJV*

Apostles are as strong on sanctification and they are on justification, regeneration and glorification.

Chapter Eight

Function 7: Distribution

Apostles are people who become "money masters," "money magnets" and "money movers." We can see the role of apostles in terms of handling the resources of the early church in the Book of Acts.

> *"Neither was there any among them that lacked: for as many as were possessors of lands or houses sold them, and brought the prices of the things that were sold, And laid them down at the apostles' feet: and distribution was made unto every man according as he had need." Acts 4:34-35 KJV*

God entrusts his apostles with a "great grace" that attracts finances that are to be gathered for use in meeting the needs of God's people and spreading the gospel to the far reaches of earth. Apostles have a "great care" for the needy among God's people as well.

> *"Now concerning the collection for the saints, as I have given order to the churches of Galatia, even so do ye. Upon the first day of the week let every one of you lay by him in store, as God hath prospered him, that there be no gatherings when I come. And when I come, whomsoever ye shall approve by your letters, them will I send to bring your liberality unto Jerusalem." 1 Corinthians 16:1-3 KJV*

Since apostles have roles of rulership and governance within the church, they manifest a "kingly anointing" that attracts finances. Jesus, operating as an apostle during his earthly ministry with a "kingly anointing," attracted great wealth. Many would have us believe that Jesus was financially destitute while on earth, the son of a lowly carpenter. However, money began to flow to Jesus from the time of his birth in Bethlehem.

> *"And when they were come into the house, they saw the young child with Mary his mother, and fell down, and worshipped him: and when they had opened their treasures, they presented unto him gifts; gold, and frankincense and myrrh." Matthew 2:11 KJV*

When Jesus began his ministry, finances began to flow to

him, enabling him to take 12 men and their families under his care for all their needs.

> *"And certain women, which had been healed of evil spirits and infirmities, Mary called Magdalene, out of whom went seven devils, and Joanna the wife of Chuza Herod's steward, and Susanna, and MANY OTHERS, which ministered unto him of their substance (property and possessions). Luke 8:2-3 KJV*

Jesus had quite a large "partner base" of support and needed Judas to serve as his "treasurer." Obviously, Jesus had some earthly treasure since he needed a "treasurer."

Because of his apostolic ministry and kingly anointing he was able to pay his taxes, support his followers and conduct a large ministry reaching thousands.

Apostles are to be "distributors" of the resources God provides according to God's will. The poor are to be cared for along with widows and orphans. New churches are to be planted, Kingdom business started and mission bases established among the nations. The gospel must be printed and broadcast thru every medium available thru modern technology. *God's will is God's bill*, and apostles are primary stewards on behalf of the Kingdom of God.

Apostles often manifest a "Joseph Anointing," who was himself prepared to steward the riches of Egypt in order to provide for God's people in times of need. God was with

Joseph and prepared him for this assignment thru all his trials and setbacks, proving his loyalty and integrity so that when the time of promotion came, he would be able to handle the responsibilities involved in the leadership role God had chosen him to fulfill. Apostles are often taken thru the type of "spiritual training" Joseph experienced starting with great prophetic vision, character development with seeming setbacks and disappointments. As someone correctly stated about Joseph's journey, it was from "The Pit to the Palace."

> *"He sent a man before them, even Joseph, who was sold for a servant: Whose feet they hurt with fetters: he was laid in iron: Until the time that his word came: the word of the Lord tried him. The king sent and loosed him; even the ruler of the people, and let him go free. He made him lord of his house, and ruler of all his substance: To bind his princes at his pleasure; and teach his senators wisdom." Psalm 105:17-22 KJV*

The apostolic ministry of the End Time Church will manifest an "apothecary" of anointing that has been deposited in them thru God ordained relationships and time spent in the "winepress" of preparation. This "mixture of anointing" includes "Elijah Anointing," "Kingly Anointing" and "Joseph Anointing" to fulfill God's purposes.

Chapter Nine

Function 8: Manifestation

An aspect of the apostolic ministry in evidence in the New Testament was the "manifestation" of miraculous power to heal and deliver people as Jesus Himself had done. Some sincere people have taught that these "signs and wonders" ceased with the first "twelve apostles" and that today all we need are the sacred Scriptures.

> *"Verily, verily, I say unto you, He that believeth on me, the works that I do shall he do also; and greater works than these shall he do; because I go unto my Father. John 14:12 KJV*

The "works of Christ" are categorized in Jesus' statement

to John's disciples, who was himself awaiting execution in prison and questioning the identity of Jesus the Messiah.

> *"Now when John had heard in the prison the works of Christ, he sent two of his disciples, And said unto him, Art thou he that should come, or do we look for another? Jesus answered and said unto them, Go and shew John again those things which ye do hear and see: The blind receive their sight, and the lame walk, the lepers are cleansed, and the deaf hear, the dead are raised up, and the poor have the gospel preached to them." Matthew 11:2-5 KJV*

The "greater works" Jesus referred to are works He had not done Himself during his earthly ministry. He told them that they would "do the works He did," and "greater works." I believe He is referring to the greater work of "regeneration" and "filling with the Spirit." Jesus' ministry was limited to the realm of physical healing, deliverance from demons and miracles that involved defying the natural laws; walking on water, multiplying food supply, changing water to wine, etc. No one was "born again" and "filled with the Spirit with evidence of speaking in tongues" until after the resurrection of Christ. These are the "greater works" because they affect the "eternal and greater part of man," his spirit being.

Remember what Jesus said about John the Baptist,

> *"Verily I say unto you, Among them that are born of women there hath not risen a greater*

> *than John the Baptist: notwithstanding he that is least in the kingdom of heaven is greater than he." Matthew 11:11 KJV*

He that is "born of women" is only "once born," but he that is "twice born" is greater, "born of the flesh and of the spirit" (John 3:3-6). Jesus is saying that anyone "born again" is greater than John the Baptist because they are "in the kingdom of heaven." John had not yet been "born again" since Christ had not yet risen from the dead as the "firstborn of many brethren." Some would say that the "greater works" are more important now and that we just need to "get people saved" and if God wills, He can heal and deliver those who need it but that is not an important ministry of the Church today. But Jesus said that his followers would do both, "the works He did" and "greater works." Salvation is for the whole man, spirit, soul and body. In fact, it is doing the "works of Jesus" that will open the doors for "greater works." When we manifest the miraculous power to heal and deliver, people will respond with the desire to be saved and filled with the Spirit.

> *"And the very God of peace sanctify you wholly; and I pray God your whole spirit and soul and body be preserved blameless unto the coming of our Lord Jesus Christ" 1 Thessalonians 5:23 KJV*

Apostles are to continue in the manifestation of miraculous power and mentor the church in doing the same. It was the manifestation of power that drew multitudes to Christ then, and the same is needed today to convince people that Jesus

Christ is truly risen and glorified. We see this principle working effectively in the Book of Acts.

> *"And by the hands of the apostles were many signs and wonders wrought among the people; (and they were all with one accord in Solomon's porch. And of the rest durst no man join himself to them: but the people magnified them. And believers were the more added to the Lord, multitudes both of men and women.)" Acts 5:12-14 KJV*

Notice the three stages to increase in this passage:

- ***Manifestation*** - verse 12 "And by the hands of the apostles were many signs and wonders."
- ***Magnification*** - verse 13 "but the people magnified them."
- ***Multiplication*** - verse 14 "multitudes of men and women."

As the apostles manifested the power of God, the believers "magnified them," they went and told everybody what was happening, and multitudes came and got saved. This is divine pattern for apostolic ministry until Jesus returns.

Paul's apostolic ministry was also confirmed by signs and wonders, and he was not one of the "original twelve," but was an "ascension apostle" as are all of today's apostles.

"And God wrought special miracles by the hands of Paul: So that from his body were brought unto the sick handkerchiefs or aprons, and the diseases departed from them, and the evil spirits went out of them." Acts 19:11-12 KJV

"How shall we escape, if we neglect so great salvation; which at the first began to be spoken by the Lord, and was confirmed unto us by them that heard him; God also bearing them witness, both with signs and wonders, and with divers miracles, and gifts of the Holy Ghost, according to his own will?" Hebrews 2:3-4 KJV

Chapter Ten

Function 9: Generation

Apostles are "generational" in their thinking. When Paul was speaking to his spiritual son, Timothy, he referred to "four generations" of potential disciples of Jesus Christ.

> *"And the things that you have heard from me among many witnesses, commit these to faithful men who will be able to teach others also." 2 Timothy 2:2 NKJV*

Notice the four generations of learners:

1st generation - "Paul"

2nd generation - "Timothy"

3rd generation - “faithful men”

4th generation - “others”

Apostles are “multi-generational” thinkers because they are “spiritual fathers” who are seeking to raise a “spiritual family” of sons and daughters to carry on the vision of ministry from one generation to another. God is a “family God," He is a “Father” who created mankind to have a family to shed His Love upon. The greatest expression of our God is His “Father’s Heart," which Jesus revealed during his earth walk.

> *“No one has seen God at any time. The only begotten [a]Son, who is in the bosom of the Father, He has declared Him. John 1:18 NKJV*

> *“He who has seen me has seen the Father.” John 14:9 NKJV*

The greatest expression of the Kingdom of God on earth will be the Family of God, when it is fully restored and functioning with spiritual fathers, mothers, sons and daughters. God promised that the “spirit of Elijah’ would come to prepare the church for the final harvest and return of Jesus Christ. These things would occur as a result of the “restoration of God’s Spiritual Family” on earth.

> *“Behold, I will send you Elijah the prophet before the coming of the great and dreadful day of the Lord. And he will turn the hearts of the fathers to the children, and the hearts of the children*

> *to their fathers, lest I come and strike the earth with a curse." Malachi 4:5-6 NKJV*

Apostle Paul speaks of God's End Time Family to the Ephesians and enumerates the qualities that will be revealed in it. The "Family of God" was a great theme of apostolic writings so it stands to reason that teaching on the "spiritual family" will be among the messages that apostles bring to the Body of Christ today.

> *"For this cause I bow my knees unto the Father of our Lord Jesus Christ, Of whom the whole family in heaven and earth is named, That he would grant you, according to the riches of his glory, to be strengthened with might by his Spirit in the inner man; That Christ may dwell in your hearts by faith; that ye, being rooted and grounded in love, May be able to comprehend with all saints what is the breadth, and length, and depth, and height; And to know the love of Christ, which passeth knowledge, that ye might be filled with all the fulness of God. Now unto him that is able to do exceeding abundantly above all that we ask or think, according to the power that worketh in us, Unto him be glory in the church by Christ Jesus throughout all ages, world without end. Amen." Ephesians 3:14-21 KJV*

Paul spoke often of his role as "spiritual father" to his sons in ministry. Being an "apostle" involves more than "gifting," it includes the wisdom and love of a "father" that exists to serve the needs of the family. Someone can be gifted with an apostolic grace, but may not have matured to the level of being a "spiritual father." One cannot have a "fathers heart" who has not themselves been a "son or daughter" to someone who fulfilled a "paternal role" in their life. We develop the heart of a father by being "fathered." Those who go out in ministry based solely upon "gifting" and "anointing," but have not enjoyed a relationship with a spiritual father, will usually "use people" to build their church, rather than using their church to build people. "Religious leadership" is the result of ministering only from "gifts" and not from a "father's heart," formed in us thru an intimate relationship with someone who represents God's heart to us. When we have allowed the kind of intimacy in relationship that allows others to "see into me" and reveal the issues of heart that we are often blind too within ourselves, we will become the kind of leader that can build a family (not just a ministry) and leave a legacy for generations.

> *"I do not write these things to shame you, but as my beloved children I warn you. For though you might have ten thousand instructors in Christ, yet you do not have many fathers; for in Christ Jesus I have begotten you through the gospel. Therefore I urge you, imitate me. 1 Corinthians 4:14-16 NKJV*

> *"as you know how we exhorted, and comforted, and charged every one of you, as a father does his own children," 1 Thessalonians 2:11 NKJV*

Spiritual fathers are those who were "faithful sons" that overcame the orphan spirit leading to independence, by serving in the ministry of another. Paul uses Timothy as the supreme example from his own ministry, of how a "servant" became a "son" to him in Christ.

> *"But I trust in the Lord Jesus to send Timotheus shortly unto you, that I also may be of good comfort, when I know your state. For I have no man likeminded, who will naturally care for your state. For all seek their own, not the things which are Jesus Christ's. But ye know the proof of him, that, as a son with the father, he hath served with me in the gospel. Him therefore I hope to send presently, so soon as I shall see how it will go with me." Philippians 2:19-23 KJV*

When we begin our walk with a spiritual father in our lives, we begin by developing the servant heart, this is where we learn to "do" things in ministry. After serving and doing, we then begin to focus on "becoming," and actually begin to reproduce the qualities of spirit that are already developed in our mentor. Jesus was both a "servant" and a "son" to his Father. As a mature son, he could say, "If you have seen me, you have seen the Father." In other words, the same qualities of spirit in God the Father were now in the Son. Jesus truly "re-presented" the Father to others, which is what a mature "spiritual son" will do. Timothy had served Paul, than as a "son" he could "re-present" Paul's same sincere interest in the Philippians. He had become "like" his spiritual father in the spiritual qualities of his life, and Paul felt safe in sending him, know that Timothy would deal with these Christians exactly as he himself would do. No surprises from an "independent spirit' that likes to "do their own thing" when given an assignment. Timothy had truly "proven himself" as spiritual son and was trusted by Paul.

Apostles are spiritual fathers and mothers to the church who reproduce themselves in the sons and daughters of ministry.

Chapter Eleven

The Release Of Apostles

RECOGNIZE THEM

"And He Himself gave some to be apostles, some prophets, some evangelists, and some pastors and teachers." Ephesians 4:11 NKJV

"Are all apostles? are all prophets? are all teachers? are all workers of miracles?" 1 Corinthians 12:29 KJV

"As You sent Me into the world, I also have sent them into the world." John 17:18 NKJV

Apostles are the same in terms of being Ambassadors,

Generals and Patriarchs of the faith, but they may differ in the sphere of ministry, they are sent to by the Lord.

As ***AMBASSADORS***, apostles are fully authorized to represent the one who sent them.

> *"And when He had called His twelve disciples to Him, He gave them power over unclean spirits, to cast them out, and to heal all kinds of sickness and all kinds of disease. Matthew 10:1 NKJV*

The Greek word "exousia," translated "power" in this verse actually means "full authority," "the right to command."

As ***GENERALS***, apostles are leaders in spiritual warfare, military strategists who train the warriors for battle.

> *"For though we walk in the flesh, we do not war after the flesh: (For the weapons of our warfare are not carnal, but mighty through God to the pulling down of strong holds;) Casting down imaginations, and every high thing that exalteth itself against the knowledge of God, and bringing into captivity every thought to the obedience of Christ;" 2 Corinthians 10:3-5 KJV*

As ***PATRIARCHS***, apostles are spiritual fathers raising up generations of spiritual sons and daughters to carry the vision of ministry. They are Abraham's with great spiritual families that have come from their spiritual loins.

Paul spoke of having a "limited sphere" which God had

appointed him. Being an apostle does not give one the right to "overstep" into another's field, or automatically give one authority in every church or ministry. Paul would not have claimed jurisdiction over a church under the care of Apostle Peter, for example.

> *"We, however, will not boast beyond measure, but within the limits of the sphere which God appointed us—a sphere which especially includes you." 2 Corinthians 10:13 NKJV*

Apostles can be sent to the Nations and primarily focus on missions, or they can be sent to the Marketplace and focus of development of Business that supplies resources into God's Kingdom advance. Apostles can be sent to the local church and raise up Networks of Local Churches that they lead and oversee. Some apostles are graced to operate in all three areas. Each one should know the limits of their God ordained sphere.

It would be easy to get confused regarding apostles if we don't understand the differences and likenesses that may appear among God called apostles. C. Peter Wagner originated the terms, "horizontal apostle" and "vertical apostle" which refer to those apostles who have "oversight of ministries" and act as a "covering" (Paul was vertical), and apostles who are horizontal (Barnabas) and serve as "big brothers" and "apostolic helps" to churches and ministries without being a covering to them.

Our ministry established a Bible College in Western Kenya in 1998 that was opened to serve all Ministries in the country regardless of affiliation. Our school has graduated leaders from over 50 different organizations of every Christian stream. There were some students who came to us without any affiliation and upon graduating they decided on joining our organization for spiritual covering. As the Founding Apostle of our ministry, I became the spiritual father to these pastors and our spiritual family was formed. A problem arose when I returned to the States, the pastors began to look for someone to be in leadership among them and the model that was most common at the time in Kenya was to ordain a "bishop" to oversee the group. I choose a man whom I had known for many years, a native Kenyan, whom I felt was trustworthy and would give them the same care I myself would, and ordained him as Bishop of our network of churches. This turned out to be a mistake and almost destroyed our ministry there when it turned out that the "Bishop" began to "lord over the pastors," not having a "fathers heart." I had to remove the man and instead, we sent a spiritual son from the US as an "ambassador apostle," a "big brother" if you will. The individual ministries we had ordained didn't need an "overseer," the pastor should be the overseer of his or her own ministry, the "bishop" of their own house. What the pastors needed was a "father" who would care for them and give them the proper counsel when they needed it. Since I was not available, we sent a "son" who could represent our heart to them, not becoming their "father," but a "big brother," a Barnabas apostle who would treat them like "family" and speak into their lives as I would if present. The model and the use of a horizontal apostle restored the family and today we are still healthy and growing while I remain the "vertical apostle" of the group.

COMMISSION THEM.

The word, "commission" means to "*order or authorize (a person or organization) to do or produce something.*" Apostles are to be "commissioned" after having given evidence of their "ambassadorial, generalship and patriarchal" abilities. Since apostles are a governmental ministry in the church, the wisdom, knowledge and experience necessary for this function takes years to develop and comes about through functioning at various other levels of ministry where the experience can be acquired. We see an example of this developmental process in King David, who first learned to "tend sheep" before becoming a ruler of God's people.

> *"Now therefore, thus shall you say to My servant David, 'Thus says the Lord of hosts: "I took you from the sheepfold, from following the sheep, to be ruler over My people, over Israel. 2 Samuel 7:8 NKJV*

David demonstrated the qualities necessary to be "ruler" of God's people, even while he was serving in his father's house as a shepherd boy. All Israel bore witness to David's capabilities and affirmed his calling from God to be King.

Apostolic Commissioning should be conducted by seasoned apostles who recognize the preparedness of an individual that God is raising up. There comes a great release of anointing and authority when commissioning occurs, and catapults a person into a new level of effectiveness. Some apostles have been prepared by the Lord in "hiding" for years and have developed fruitful ministries without the recognition of other apostles, these individuals should be identified and commissioned upon being discovered.

All "fivefold" ministry gifts that seek a "vocation" of ministry should be ordained by local church authority, however, ordination and commissioning are not one and the same. As we explained earlier in this writing, "ordination" of church leadership gives one the authorization to function within the church as examples, feeders and leaders of the flock in official capacity as elders, deacons and bishops. With regards to apostles, commissioning follows ordination as a church official and affirms the work that has been done, the character that has been developed and the anointing that has been manifested. With this in mind, a person generally doesn't begin ministry as an "apostle," even if prophecy was given to that effect. Beginning as pastor, teacher or evangelist will provide the necessary experience, wisdom and character to be recognized as an apostle.

Someone with the calling of apostle upon their life will "emerge" into the fullness of that ministry. For those called to lead churches and networks, the ministry will usually grow and the need for more leaders to be trained with it. The emerging apostle will no longer be able to "tend sheep," but will need to train the leaders, open new doors of ministry and travel away from the local church more frequently. The congregation will need to release the apostle for the functions that come with a growing ministry, and understand that others can do pastoral work and care for the sheep in their absence. Peter Wagner describes this transition as going from a “Shepherd” to a “Rancher” who has many pastures with shepherds tending each one.

Releasing apostles into the fullness of their calling involves recognition of the gift, ordination to ministry and commissioning in the right season. We are living in exciting times of restoration of all gifts and ministries of the Holy Spirit. Presently the gift of Apostle is being emphasized by the Holy Spirit and accepted by the Body of Christ, let us receive all of God's gifts and ministries for the edifying and equipping of His Church for a great final harvest.

ABOUT THE AUTHOR

John Polis was saved and filled with Holy Spirit in 1974 during the Jesus Movement. He attended Dayton Bible College and graduated with a B.A. in Biblical Studies in 1980, after which he became pastor of a Pentecostal church in West Virginia.

In 1983, John had an encounter that transitioned him into the ministry of Apostle. Afterwards, he began to travel as an Evangelist and International Bible Teacher.

Among the works established was Eldoret Bible College in Kenya, Africa, which was birthed in 1998 and has graduated over 2500 students with undergraduate and graduate degrees. Students have planted more than 600 churches throughout Africa to date, some of which have more than 5000 in attendance. John has been a television and radio host for more than 40 years and has authored 18 publications, translated into 6 languages. As President and Founder of Revival Fellowship International, John, and his wife Rebecca, have many spiritual sons and daughters in 13 states and 5 countries. John carries and imparts an Elijah Anointing to prepare the Church for discipling nations as mature sons and daughters. John serves on the Council of Elders for the International Coalition of Apostolic Leaders and is a former United States Marine, being a veteran of the Vietnam War. John and Rebecca have been married 47 years, with 4 children and 9 grandchildren.

MORE BOOKS BY JOHN POLIS

9 Apostolic Functions:
Things Apostles Do.

Built Strong:
31 Keys To Spiritual Power.

God Fathers:
How You Can Be One.

Stronger Than Satan:
Understanding Your Authority In Christ.

Victorious:
How To Face, Fight, and Finish Your Battles.

Release The River Within You:
Increasing The Anointing Flow

Put On Your Gloves:
The Five Battles Every Christian Must Win.

Apostolic Advice:
Proven Wisdom for Building Strong Foundations in the Local Church.

Recycled Believers:
Solving The Mystery of Migrating Sheep.

How To Produce Abundance In Your Life:
The Kingdom Secrets Jesus Taught His Disciples.

Biblical Headship:
Making Sense of Submission To Authority.

The Master Builder:
Wisdom for Today's Apostles

Take My Yoke Upon You:
Fulfilling Your 3 Dimensional Destiny

The Kings Are Coming:
Understanding The Kingly Anointing

BE STRONG IN THE LORD:
DISCIPLESHIP SERIES BOOKS BY JOHN POLIS

Living Unshakeable In A Shaking World:
6 Principles For Successful Kingdom Living.

Total Victory Is For You:
5 Smooth Stones To Slay Your Giants.

The Love Of God

How To Obtain Strong Faith

Spiritual Warfare:
No Place For Satan

For these and additional resources to help you in your spiritual growth, go to www.johnpolis.com.

www.ingramcontent.com/pod-product-compliance
Lightning Source LLC
LaVergne TN
LVHW020655100826
845148LV00012B/2510

* 9 7 8 1 7 3 7 7 2 3 6 7 7 *